W9-ALE-524

Dr. Mary Edwards Walker

Military Heroes

DR. MARY EDWARDS WALKER

CIVIL WAR SURGEON & MEDAL OF HONOR RECIPIENT

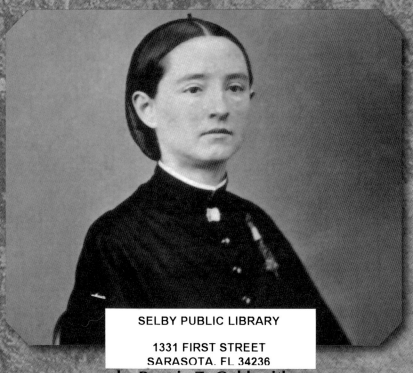

by Bonnie Z. Goldsmith

Content Consultant:
Steven D. Smith, Associate Director for Applied Research,
South Carolina Institute of Archaeology and Anthropology

ABDO
Publishing Company

CREDITS

Published by ABDO Publishing Company, 8000 West 78th Street, Edina, Minnesota 55439. Copyright © 2010 by Abdo Consulting Group, Inc. International copyrights reserved in all countries. No part of this book may be reproduced in any form without written permission from the publisher. The Essential Library™ is a trademark and logo of ABDO Publishing Company.

Printed in the United States of America,
North Mankato, Minnesota
102009
012010

 PRINTED ON RECYCLED PAPER

Editor: Amy Van Zee
Copy Editor: Paula Lewis
Interior Design and Production: Becky Daum
Cover Design: Becky Daum

Library of Congress Cataloging-in-Publication Data
Goldsmith, Bonnie Zucker.
  Dr. Mary Edwards Walker : Civil War surgeon & medal of honor recipient / Bonnie Z. Goldsmith.
    p. cm. — (Military heroes)
  Includes bibliographical references and index.
  ISBN 978-1-60453-966-0 (alk. paper)
  1. Walker, Mary Edwards, 1832-1919. 2. Physicians—United States—Biography—Juvenile literature. 3. Women physicians—United States—Biography—Juvenile literature. 4. Suffragists—United States—Biography—Juvenile literature. 5. United States—History—Civil War, 1861-1865—Medical care—Juvenile literature. 6. United States—History—Civil War, 1861-1865—Women—Juvenile literature. I. Title.
  R154.W18G65 2010
  610.92—dc22
  [B]
                                                2009032367

TABLE OF CONTENTS

The American Civil War began on April 12, 1861. More than 600,000 lives were lost during the war.

PRISONER OF WAR

It was April 10, 1864. The North and the South had been engaged in the bloody American Civil War for three years. Thirty-one year old Dr. Mary Edwards Walker bravely rode her horse behind enemy lines. She was the only female physician officially assigned to a Union regiment. Her regiment, the Fifty-second Ohio, was stationed at Gordon's Mills, a small town near Chattanooga, Tennessee. The Union soldiers were in fairly good health, but the Southern civilians in the area lacked food, supplies, and medical care. Walker had her commander's approval to help them.

In Enemy Territory

Walker usually traveled with two officers and two medical assistants. They were each armed, and she carried two pistols in her saddle. At times, however, she volunteered to travel alone into dangerous areas to treat the sick. When she did, she left her guns behind so that, if she were stopped, the Confederates would see she came in peace. On this day, alone and unarmed, she went too far into Confederate territory and was stopped by a sentry. Suspicious, he took her captive. Only two months after becoming an official Union physician, Walker was a prisoner of war.

Walker was taken to Dalton, Georgia. There, she boarded a train for Richmond, Virginia, the capital of the Confederacy. The 700-mile (1,127-km) journey would take a full week.

At stops along the way, crowds gathered to stare at the "Yankee lady physician in bloomers."[1] Unlike most women at the time, Walker wore trousers. The pants were part of a blue surgeon's uniform she had designed for herself, which also included an officer's coat and hat.

Walker believed that women's long, heavy skirts were unhealthy. Her clothes gave her the freedom of movement she needed to practice her profession. However, society at that time accepted pants for men only. A female physician, particularly one who wore pants, was subject to insults and ridicule.

A THING

Her captors were annoyed by Walker. One Confederate captain wrote: "This morning we were all amused and disgusted too at the sight of a *thing* that nothing but the debased and the depraved Yankee nation could produce—'a female doctor.'"[2] Southern Brigadier General William M. Gardner was in charge of Walker's case. He lectured her on the importance of dressing as a woman should. He ridiculed her insistence on participating in the war.

Walker was taken to Castle Thunder prison in Richmond. The officials there were hoping to send her back to the North in a prisoner exchange. But by 1864, the process of exchanging prisoners had become complicated. Both sides squabbled over terms.

CASTLE THUNDER

Formerly a private residence, Castle Thunder was a large, brick building. It reportedly came by its name because its previous owner was known as Mistress Thunder for her bad temper.

After the days of Mistress Thunder, the building had been a tobacco warehouse. During the Civil War, it

Southern Prisons

When the Civil War began in 1861, relatively few prisoners were taken. Those who were captured were held at forts, warehouses, jails, and other buildings. Captives from both armies were sometimes exchanged. The Confederacy, in particular, could not afford to feed prisoners, so the South pressed the Lincoln administration to agree on terms for exchanging prisoners. But by 1863, the two sides quarreled about conditions—particularly the South's brutal treatment of black prisoners—and formal prisoner exchanges stopped. This led to overcrowded, undersupplied prisons.

Conditions at Southern prisons were appalling. Most were overcrowded. Captives died of disease, starvation, and brutality. Some prisons offered no shelter from the sun and rain. Guards were usually untrained and unsupervised. The Confederate camp in Andersonville, in southwest Georgia, stands out as the worst. There, 13,000 of the 45,000 prisoners died. After the war, the commandant of Andersonville was charged with war crimes and executed.

As the war went on, the Confederacy could not feed or shelter its own soldiers adequately, let alone treat prisoners humanely. In addition, prisoners' infections and wounds were not treated properly. As a result of her time at Castle Thunder, Walker developed lasting health problems.

Castle Thunder prison in Richmond, Virginia, circa 1865

housed criminals, Confederate deserters, prisoners of war, spies, and a few women. Castle Thunder was overcrowded and dirty. Poor airflow led to foul smells. Most prisoners slept on ragged blankets or piles of straw, and no outdoor exercise was allowed. Many of the inmates had been sentenced to death. Executions took place in the prison yard—in full view of the prisoners inside.

Walker's mattress swarmed with insects, and rats raced along the floors during the night. Captain George W. Alexander commanded the prison with brutality. Dressed in black and with his huge dog, Nero, by his side, he patrolled Castle Thunder shouting commands and threats. In 1863, he had been investigated by the Confederate government because of complaints about his harsh style and severe punishments. Alexander was eventually cleared of the charges. In his defense, he claimed that the prisoners were vicious and difficult to control.

Many guards, too, were brutal and amused themselves by harassing the prisoners. Sentries facing the yard were known to fire at any Northern prisoner who appeared at one of the barred windows. Later in her life, Walker told about a guard firing at her as she stood in the doorway of her cell, just missing her head. This and other incidents were dismissed as accidents.

Letters Home

To reassure her family, Walker lied about the horrendous conditions at Castle Thunder: "I hope you are not grieving about me because I am a prisoner of war. I am living in a three-story brick 'castle,' with plenty to eat, and a clean bed to sleep in. I have a roommate, a young lady. . . . The officers are gentlemanly and kind, and it will not be long before I am exchanged."[3]

A Persistent Woman

At one point during her time as a prisoner, Walker became very sick and believed she needed fresh eggs to survive. Although getting extra rations was against the rules, she persuaded a clerk to smuggle eggs to her.

A COURAGEOUS PRISONER

The muggy heat, combined with the bad smells, made life as a prisoner hard to bear. A fellow prisoner remembered Walker sitting at an open window with a fan in one hand and an American flag in the other. She deeply loved her country. When three young Union prisoners were marched into Richmond, Walker saluted them from the balcony of the jail.

Walker was a courageous and outspoken prisoner. She persuaded authorities to add wheat bread to the prisoners' meager diet and to serve fresh cabbage several times a week. She wrote many letters demanding her release. After four months in the prison, during a prisoner exchange, Walker left Castle Thunder wearing her trousers. After the war, she recounted how one official had told her he might be more sympathetic if she dressed like a proper lady. She told him that men had no right to tell women what to do or what to wear.

A LIFE OF SERVICE

During the Civil War, Walker endured bloody battlefields and crude hospitals, as well as the scorn of male military and medical authorities. For most of the war, the army refused to pay or officially employ her. Nevertheless, she continued to serve soldiers and their families. After the war, she lived the rest of her long life dedicated to patriotic service and social reform, despite health problems caused by her time at Castle Thunder.

Walker was one of the first female physicians in the United States. She was also an early women's rights activist and the only woman ever to be awarded the Congressional Medal of Honor. She spoke and wrote about the dangers of alcohol and tobacco. She addressed the need for women to hold more power in society and the need for everyone to have meaningful, fairly paid work.

Stubborn, proud, and independent, Walker was comfortable confronting anybody in her

Describing Walker

A prison chaplain wrote sarcastically, "A prisoner . . . who excited considerable interest and amusement was Miss Dr. Mary Walker. She had a room to herself in Castle Thunder, and sometimes was permitted to stroll into the streets, where her display of Bloomer costume, blouse, trowsers [trousers] and boots secured her a following of astonished and admiring boys. She was quite chatty, and seemed rather to enjoy the notoriety of her position. She claimed to be a surgeon in the Federal army, and, I believe, had some sort of commission, or permission perhaps as hospital nurse to travel with the army."[4]

Walker on Women

In Walker's 1871 book, *Hit: Essays on Women's Rights*, she wrote:

"[W]oman is politically a slave, having no voice in making the laws by which she is governed. . . . The time is not distant when women . . . will be equal with men in all the social, and political relations of life. . . . Women cannot be deprived of God-given rights."[5]

pursuit of justice, including several presidents of the United States. In the chaos of the Civil War, the need for her medical services made her necessary. After the war, however, Walker had to fight for recognition. Although her life was filled with personal disappointments, Mary Edwards Walker remained a visible part of the women's rights movement.

Mary Edwards Walker was the only female physician to serve the Union during the Civil War.

Chapter 2

The Oswego River in Oswego, New York, was a place of commerce in the mid-nineteenth century.

AN INDEPENDENT UPBRINGING

Mary Edwards Walker was born in Oswego, New York, on November 26, 1832. The thriving city was a center for both business and culture. The Oswego River, which empties into Lake Ontario, made the area a busy commercial port. The Oswego Canal linked the Erie Canal with Lake Ontario. Boats brought salt, grain, and many other products back and forth from the town.

Oswego was also in the path of many reform movements. During the 1820s and 1830s, religious fervor brought enthusiasm for moral and social reforms. People joined groups to campaign for prison reform, abstinence from alcohol, women's rights, and an end to slavery. As the Southern states insisted on the necessity—even the social and economic good—of slavery, the nation struggled with conflict that would soon tear it apart.

Freethinking Yankee Parents

Mary's family was made of freethinking Yankees who were deeply opposed to the practice of slavery. Her father, Alvah Walker, and her mother, Vesta Whitcomb Walker, came from a long line of New Englanders. Mary's father traced his ancestry to a 1643 settler in the Plymouth Colony. After his father died, Alvah left school at 13. He went to work for a carpenter to help support his mother and seven younger siblings. When his mother remarried, Alvah began traveling. He kept a diary of his work, noting house-building projects in places such as New York,

Pittsburgh, Boston, Kentucky, Mississippi, and Louisiana.

When Alvah was about 24, he returned to Boston. In 1822, he met and married Vesta, who was 20. The couple settled in Syracuse, New York, near several of Vesta's relatives, and they lived there for ten years. Their first child died only a few days after birth. While they lived in Syracuse, they had four daughters: Vesta, Aurora, Luna, and Cynthia. To support the family, Alvah worked as a carpenter and built the first frame house in Syracuse. Occasionally, he would sketch or paint, and he was an avid reader. Recurring bouts of sickness, caused by complications from measles, led him to seek remedies by reading medical books. This reading, among other things, inspired him to avoid alcohol and tobacco.

An Inventive Father

Mary Walker's first book, *Hit*, included in its endpapers an advertisement for her father's water elevator. Patented in 1868, this device brought water from the bottom of a well and poured it quickly and easily into a pail. It could also bring water into a house.

THE MOVE TO OSWEGO

In 1832, the Walkers sold their Syracuse home. They settled on a 33-acre (13-ha) farm on the Bunker Hill Road a few miles west of Oswego, New York. Three months later, their youngest daughter was born. She was named Mary Edwards after her aunt. A year later, their last child, a son, was born. Alvah cleared the land and built a house and a barn. He also built the town's first schoolhouse on his property. All the Walker children attended the school. They were taught by their parents, who were enthusiastic about education. When Oswego opened a school, Alvah turned the building into a shop, where he built items such as wooden doors, coffins, and cabinets.

To Freedom

The Walkers' farm in Oswego was a part of the Underground Railroad, which was a system of smuggling runaway slaves from the South to freedom in Canada.

Alvah Walker was an inventive, independent man who was willing to go against society's opinions. He believed girls, as well as boys, should be well-educated. All of his children were encouraged to read and study. Mary and her sisters were raised to believe they were the equals of men. The Walkers also stressed the importance of good health, exercise, and diet. Both parents opposed the current fashion of corsets and stays that cinched a woman's waist so tightly she could hardly breathe. Furthermore, they expected all the children—their son and their five daughters—to participate fully in farm chores. The girls could not work efficiently wearing long, heavy skirts. Mary, a small, slender, energetic girl

An advertisement for a popular brand of nineteenth-century corset

with long curls, learned from her earliest days to be sensible about what she wore. Later, she became an impassioned crusader for women's right to dress as they pleased.

The Walkers encouraged open discussions of the events of the day. In particular, they followed the growing divisions between the North and the

South. Mary was 16 when the first women's rights convention was held in the United States in Seneca Falls, New York. The convention was approximately 50 miles (80 km) from Oswego. One participant at Seneca Falls, Amelia Jenks Bloomer, was a leading advocate of dress reform for women. The event concluded with a declaration that all people—not just men—were created equal. Mary's family likely read about and discussed the event.

When she was 18, Mary attended Falley Seminary as her sisters had. She studied subjects such as math, philosophy, grammar, physiology, and hygiene. In January 1852, when Mary was 19, she was hired to teach school in a nearby village. Mary was determined to save her meager salary for medical school. In Oswego, Alvah Walker had served as a self-taught country doctor. Mary had read her father's medical books. She had seen him care for sick and injured farmhands and townspeople. Her upbringing convinced her that she could and should pursue whatever profession she chose.

MEDICAL SCHOOL

At that time, however, there were few women's colleges of any kind. The medical profession was particularly unwelcoming to women. Details about the human body were believed indecent for women to learn, and medical education was considered too difficult for their brains to grasp. The first woman to earn a medical degree in the United States, Elizabeth Blackwell, had graduated from New York's Geneva Medical College in 1849, when Mary was 17. Blackwell's achievement had not led to a greater acceptance of women in medicine. At the few schools that accepted women, the environment was so unfriendly that only the strongest-willed women managed to graduate.

Medicine at that time was just starting to become a profession requiring graduation from a medical school. However, doctors knew little about the causes of disease. They usually made diagnoses without using a thermometer or stethoscope and without taking the patient's pulse. Doctors practicing traditional, or "regular," medicine treated patients by drawing blood or blistering the skin. They would use toxic substances, such as mercury. Some of these treatments would kill the patient. Less drastic, "reform" medicine emerged in opposition to these extreme measures. It treated disease using water, exercise, or special diets.

In December 1853, when Mary was 21, she was admitted to Syracuse Medical College. Syracuse was an eclectic school. It taught a variety of reform approaches to medicine. Mary was probably familiar with these methods from observing her father's doctoring. Over a span of two years, Mary took basic courses in anatomy, surgery, pathology, obstetrics, physiology, pharmacy, and chemistry. Between terms, students worked with practicing physicians. The program was

Elizabeth Blackwell

Geneva Medical College, where Elizabeth Blackwell studied, was approximately 50 miles (80 km) from Oswego. Like Mary, Blackwell began her career as a teacher. She became interested in medicine, particularly the need for female physicians to care for female patients. After many rejections, Blackwell was accepted at Geneva only because the male students, who were asked to decide whether to admit her or not, thought her application was a hoax. She graduated first in her class.

During the Civil War, Blackwell and her sister, also a physician, helped to organize the Women's Central Association of Relief, which trained nurses for war service. This organization inspired the creation of the U.S. Sanitary Commission (USSC) in June 1861. The USSC coordinated the volunteer efforts of Northern women. During the war, these women lobbied Congress for medical reform, raised money, opened veterans' homes, and sent nurses into battle zones.

Nothing is recorded about a meeting between Walker and Blackwell, but both women worked in Washington DC at the beginning of the war. Each offered her services to the Union, and each worked in hospitals. Blackwell may well have known about Mary, whose independent ideas about dress and women's rights were sometimes reported in Washington DC and New York newspapers.

Healing Methods

In the nineteenth century, nontraditional medical schools taught various approaches to healing. Hydrotherapy, for example, soothed pains and treated diseases with water. Thomsonianism used herbs and other plants to treat disease. Homeopathy stressed the use of drugs in gradually increasing amounts, rather than traditional medicine's massive doses. Eclectic schools, such as Syracuse Medical College, taught what were considered the best of the various approaches.

intensive and quite thorough. The only woman in her class, Mary received her medical degree in June 1855. She then resolved to make her living practicing medicine.

But Mary soon encountered major obstacles. Because she had attended a nontraditional medical school, some saw her as a quack. In addition, she was female. And her confident, uncompromising personality was not considered appropriate for a woman. She was determined, however, to use her medical training to help those around her, so she set out to do just that.

Mary Edwards Walker faced many difficulties as she attempted to secure a job as a physician.

This cartoon depicts schools of eclectic medicine as "diploma mills."
Many were skeptical about the training given at eclectic schools.

MEDICINE, MARRIAGE, AND DRESS REFORM

ary Edwards Walker's lifelong battle for equality began with dress reform. Throughout her life, she insisted that the long, heavy skirts and tight corsets favored by fashionable women were not only uncomfortable but also unhealthy.

Long skirts collected filth from the streets. Tight undergarments compressed the vital organs, deformed the bones, and interfered with breathing and blood circulation.

What women wore was not a trivial matter in the nineteenth-century United States. One of the most controversial issues in the women's rights movement was dress reform, as dress defined one's place in society. Trousers equaled maleness, and maleness equaled independence. Women who dared to wear trousers were seen as frightening, ridiculous, and indecent. Even when a woman's trousers were almost entirely hidden by her skirt, they were considered a threat to the entire structure of society.

Dress reform went public in the spring of 1851. Elizabeth Smith Miller, a middle-class woman from New York, created a national sensation when she began to appear

The Fashionable Woman

In the 1840s and 1850s, women's dresses emphasized a curvy figure and a tiny waist. To achieve this, women laced themselves into corsets so tight that fainting was common.

Corsets also helped support the weight of large, heavy, bell-shaped skirts stiffened with rolls of horsehair in the lining. The skirts were supported by as many as seven starched underskirts, called petticoats, fastened at the waist. Including undergarments, some outfits had 12 or more layers of fabric wrapped around a woman's waist.

In 1856, hoopskirts were introduced. Made of steel wires, these petticoats looked like cages and supported wide skirts. These hoopskirts took up entire paths, and their trains dragged through the dust and mud.

in an outfit she had designed. She wore pantaloons under a dress that fell slightly below the knees. She said these clothes were more healthful than long, heavy dresses and made it easier for her to work in her garden.

Miller's cousin, reformer Elizabeth Cady Stanton, copied Miller's outfit. So did their mutual friend Amelia Jenks Bloomer. In the June 1851 issue of Bloomer's magazine, the *Lily*, Bloomer wrote about the physical dangers of conventional clothing to women's spines, lungs, and other internal

The Women's Movement

In the early 1800s, women in the United States could not vote, hold public office, or serve on juries. Few women received any higher education. Women could not work in most trades or professions. When they did work, they labored in places such as mills and factories in the industrializing Northeast. They were paid less than men doing the same jobs, and their fathers or husbands often took their earnings. Married women lost legal control of all money and property to their husbands. Wives could not testify against their husbands in court, sue for divorce, or gain custody of their children.

But in the many reform movements of the 1830s and 1840s, women began to take more active roles. Women led the fight for more public schools, prison reform, better treatment of mentally ill people, and temperance. The abolitionist movement attracted many women, and some anti-slavery groups were made up entirely of women.

The women's rights movement was inspired by the abolitionist movement. Women working to end slavery pointed out the parallels between the powerless state of slaves and the powerless state of women. Two leading reformers in the growing women's rights movement were Lucretia Mott and Elizabeth Cady Stanton.

organs. Though most women's rights advocates called the new clothing "freedom dress" or "reform dress," the publicity Bloomer provided led to Miller's outfit becoming known as "bloomers." Dress reform was clearly linked to the women's movement. Newspapers ridiculed the clothing and the reformist women who wore it.

During medical school, Walker developed her own version of bloomers. Instead of pantaloons, she wore straight, tailored trousers supported by suspenders. Over the trousers, she wore a long-sleeved, high-necked, loose-waisted dress that fell just below the knees. She never again wore long skirts, although her clothes brought her ridicule wherever she went. Later in life, she declared, "I don't wear men's clothes. I wear my own clothes."[1]

Bloomers

The Bloomer outfit usually consisted of a knee-length dress over long pants. This ensemble was previously called pantaloons. Although other women had worn pantaloons, the ensemble began to be called bloomers as they became well-known.

SIBYL

In the 1850s, Walker met a woman who gave her an outlet for her dress-reform ideas. Dr. Lydia Sayer Hasbrouck had much in common with Walker. Both were

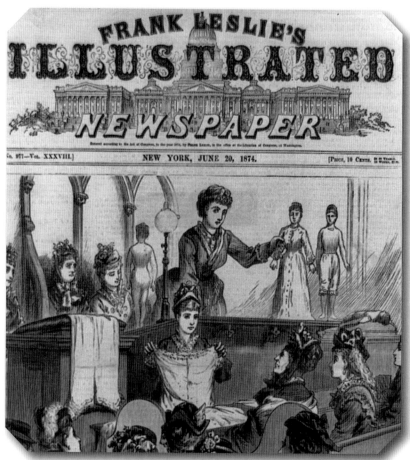

An illustration of an 1874 women's dress reform meeting in Boston, Massachusetts

nontraditional physicians, and both believed that popular women's clothing was harmful to their health. Hasbrouck and Walker continued to wear reform dress throughout their lives. Late in 1856, Walker began subscribing to Hasbrouck's new reform magazine, *Sibyl: A Review of the Tastes, Errors and Fashions of Society*. *Sibyl* published articles by men and women on all aspects of reform, but it was particularly noted for its coverage of women's rights issues. The magazine soon became the main voice of the National Dress Reform Association.

Walker wrote a letter to the magazine on January 1, 1857, welcoming news of a dress-reform convention to be held in Canastota, New York, near Syracuse. At the convention, Walker spoke about and demonstrated the most efficient reform dress. In her second letter to the magazine, she reported on the convention, and she continued to contribute letters and articles to the publication. In December 1857, *Sibyl* announced that Walker had begun lecturing on dress reform. These lectures became an important source of income for her. She argued that women needed to understand the dangers restrictive clothing posed to their health. At the 1860 meeting of the National Dress Reform Association, Walker was elected one of nine vice presidents.

FINDING HER WAY

Although Walker believed passionately in dress reform, she was also trying to become a successful physician. In 1855, Walker decided to begin her medical career in Columbus, Ohio, where her father's sister had settled. However, Walker could not get a practice started in Columbus and returned to New York after a few months.

Walker's return to New York may have followed a proposal of marriage. At medical school, she had been courted by classmate Albert Miller. He was known for being an orator and freethinker. In the fall of 1855, they were married at the Walker home in an unconventional ceremony. Mary wore trousers and a coat. Her vows did not include what she called "the tyrannical custom of promising to 'honor and obey.'"[2] Furthermore, she insisted on keeping her own name, although she sometimes referred to herself as Dr. Miller-Walker.

Miller invited his new wife to join his practice in Rome, New York. They lived and worked together happily for a while. Then Walker learned that her husband had been unfaithful. By the early 1860s, they were separated, and their divorce was final in 1869. In 1865, Miller had written a letter to Walker's brother-

Married Names

In her 1871 book, *Hit*, Walker commented about women's married names: "A woman's name is as dear to her as a man's is to him, and custom ought, and will prevail, where each will keep their own names when they marry, and allow the children at a certain age to decide which name they will prefer."[3]

in-law inquiring after her well-being. Walker, however, persisted in calling him a "villain. . . . the vile Miller."[4] She would never remarry.

On Her Own

Divorce was rare for a woman at that time. Being divorced meant that Walker lost social status and had no financial protection. She knew what she had lost, and the breakup colored her view of life from then on. Walker felt that the institution of marriage was a true blessing, and when her own ended in divorce, she was bitter and angry.

After moving to an apartment, Walker took out a notice in the Rome *Sentinel* announcing her new location and office hours for her medical practice. Alone and with rent to pay, she traveled in a horse and buggy to pull teeth, deliver babies, and provide first aid.

Determined to Serve the Union

As Walker struggled to earn a living as a speaker and physician, the United States inched closer to civil war. As the daughter of abolitionist parents,

Divorce

Divorce was difficult for a woman to obtain in the nineteenth century. Walker wrote: "To be deprived of a Divorce is like being shut up in a prison because some one attempted to kill you. . . . If it is right to be legally married, it is right to be legally Divorced."[5]

Walker anxiously followed the news as the country split over the issues of slavery and states' rights. She read about John Brown's raid to seize a U.S. arsenal at Harpers Ferry, West Virginia, in October 1859. In 1860, she read news of the election of Abraham Lincoln as president of the United States. She heard about the secession of South Carolina in December, 1860, and how other Southern states followed suit. Then, in April 1861, she read the news everyone had been dreading: Confederate guns had fired on Fort Sumter, South Carolina. The Civil War had begun.

The war created an urgent need for physicians. Dr. Mary Walker hoped the Union's critical need for doctors would override discrimination against female physicians and doctors trained in nontraditional medical schools. She also expected that her dress habits would be seen as practical for her work. But such was not the case.

Bloomers consisted of pants worn under a skirt. Mary Edwards Walker considered similar attire appropriate for her work as a physician.

Chapter 4

Approximately 3,000 Union troops died during the First Battle of Bull Run.

To Be of Service

Dr. Mary Walker was nearly 29 when she arrived in Washington DC in October 1861. A few months earlier, the First Battle of Bull Run had raged a short distance outside the city. Walker was ready to use her medical training to serve her country. At that time, Washington DC was a shabby, crime-filled city. It had only six government buildings, including the unfinished Capitol building. Most streets were open sewers. Diseases such as cholera, typhoid, dysentery, and malaria were common.

Meanwhile, troops were everywhere in the city, and the army had almost no medical facilities there. The U.S. War Department faced a shortage of medical help, hospitals, and supplies. Public buildings, churches, private homes, and even tents were all used as hospitals.

SEEKING A COMMISSION

Walker reported to the U.S. Army's Medical Department seeking an official commission as a doctor. She carried letters of recommendation from two male physicians who attested to her training, competence, and high moral standards. Women attempting

Bull Run

The First Battle of Bull Run was an important Confederate victory. In July 1861, General Irvin McDowell and more than 30,000 Union troops were sent to attack Confederate forces waiting outside Washington DC. Confederate troops, commanded by General Pierre G. T. Beauregard and General Joseph E. Johnston, met the troops in battle near a creek called Bull Run. Initially, the Union seemed to be winning. But determined Southern troops under General Thomas J. "Stonewall" Jackson sent McDowell's army fleeing back to Washington DC. The various reporters, congressmen, and other civilians who had turned out to see what they thought would be an easy Union victory also made a hasty retreat to Washington DC.

to practice medicine often had their moral character questioned. Many people felt it was improper for women to work in army hospitals with male patients. When Walker made her application, the men were "stunned but not speechless . . . for no other woman had dared suggest such a thing, and the Surgeon General, rejecting the application, implied that it had never occurred to him that one would."[1]

Walker would probably have met with resistance even if she had been male. All doctors trained in nontraditional schools were viewed with suspicion. Still, in 1861, she managed to secure an unpaid volunteer position as assistant to Dr. J. N. Green at the Indiana Hospital. This hospital was crowded into a part of the United States Patent Office. The facility was called the Indiana Hospital because it mostly served wounded and sick troops from Indiana. There, Walker began one of her most important, self-appointed tasks. She became a friend to soldiers and their families.

THE INDIANA HOSPITAL

The Indiana Hospital cared for approximately 80 patients at a time. Green, who was working alone after the death of his assistant, desperately needed help. He was impressed with Walker's credentials and unconcerned about her gender. While she continued to campaign for an army commission, she worked as an unofficial and unpaid ward doctor. Walker prescribed medicine and evaluated patients for treatment. She met ambulances to be sure no one with smallpox was placed with other patients, and she answered calls for help. Her assertive personality was an advantage during wartime. If she saw a need or a problem, she acted. Walker slept in a hospital alcove and shared hospital rations with the few nurses.

Walker's main desire was to relieve Green of some of his burdens. Green was grateful and wrote to Surgeon General Clement A. Finley and asked that he find a way to pay Walker. Green wrote, "I need and desire her assistance here very much believing as I do that she is well qualified for the position."[2] Walker carried the letter to Finley herself, but he told her he could not appoint a woman. She then presented her credentials to the assistant surgeon general, Dr. Robert C. Wood. He was sympathetic but could not override

"Incidents Connected with the Army"

Walker never wrote an autobiography or even a complete account of her Civil War experiences. She did leave 38 pages of unordered, undated, typed notes, however. She called them "Incidents Connected with the Army." Much of what historians know about her service comes from these pages, which are now kept at Syracuse University.

his superior. At one point, Green offered Walker part of his salary, but she declined. She told him he needed to provide for his wife and children.

Tireless Service

As Walker had no official duties at the Indiana Hospital, she was free to assist soldiers and their families whenever a need arose. Walker often wrote letters for soldiers and sat at bedsides keeping lonely men company.

WITHOUT AN INCOME

Walker had to find a way to support herself. By early 1862, she had returned to New York. Before going home, she went to New York City and studied at the Hygeia Therapeutic College. This unconventional medical school stressed hygiene and natural cures for disease. Walker received a diploma from this school, perhaps in an attempt to strengthen her credentials. But another nontraditional school would not increase her chances of securing a military commission.

In October 1862, Walker went back to Oswego to live with her family. She earned a little money by giving lectures and writing articles on dress reform and on her Washington DC experiences. But her intense patriotism and desire to be of service drove her back to the war, which was continuing longer than either side had expected.

General Burnside, right, eventually became commander of the Union army.

BATTLEFIELD DOCTOR, WARD CONDUCTOR

Walker returned to Washington DC prepared to offer her assistance again without pay. In November, she headed for Warrenton, Virginia, where the Army of the Potomac was stationed under General Ambrose Burnside. The army was suffering from an outbreak of typhoid fever. They had no medicine and no supplies. With the permission of the camp's medical director, she tended to the sickest soldiers. Walker tore up her own nightgown to make strips of cloth for bathing the faces of feverish soldiers.

Walker also managed to convince the authorities that the sickest patients needed to be moved to Washington DC for treatment and that she should go with them. On November 15, 1862, General Burnside gave her written permission to do so. She boarded the northbound train with her patients, convincing the engineer that her orders needed to be followed. Once she was on board, Walker walked from car to car making the soldiers as comfortable as possible. Walker had impressed male authorities with her commitment to the Union cause and her medical skills.

On to Fredericksburg

Next, Walker traveled to Fredericksburg,

A Volunteer

Walker showed much compassion while serving in hospitals. Her service also may have shown her determination. Some speculate that she continued to volunteer at the hospital to prove how serious she was about her desire to acquire a paid position.

Walker demonstrated a common belief in the importance of female self-sacrifice and service to others. Walker was devoted to her patients and relished every opportunity to serve them. She performed with skill as well. A newspaper reporter who watched her wrote:

> Dressed in male habiliments [clothes], with the exception of a girlish-looking straw hat, decked off with an ostrich feather, with a petite figure and feminine features. . . . [S]he can amputate a limb with the skill of an old surgeon, and administer medicine equally as well.

He also reported that "the lady referred to is exceedingly popular among the soldiers in the hospital, and is undoubtedly doing much good."[3]

Virginia, where the Union army had suffered a major defeat in December 1862. Thousands had died or been wounded. Among the rotting corpses, men with bloody wounds cried for help. Walker described the case of a man whose skull had been pierced. Through the hole, she could see his brain. She comforted a dying drummer boy who had lost both legs. She learned he was the only child of a widow in Washington DC. Walker searched for the woman and told her the sad news of her son's death. Later, she arranged a job for the widow to help shell-shocked soldiers in an asylum.

Preston King was a doctor in Fredericksburg. He saw the injustice of Walker's labors being rewarded with nothing but food and a tent. He wrote to Secretary of War Edwin Stanton on her behalf, detailing her services and asking that she be paid. However, as King told Walker, there was no law allowing pay for a woman doctor working without a commission. Walker believed that "Congress should assign women to duty in the Army with compensation . . . averring [proving] that patriotism has no sex."[4]

Despite this setback, Walker wore the green sash of a surgeon around her waist whenever she was in

Private Counseling

In "Incidents Connected with the Army," Walker wrote: "I did not wish to be unprofessional and say anything to any other medical officer's patients . . . but . . . I had a little experience and observation regarding the inability of some of the ward surgeons to diagnose properly, and truthfully I considered that I had a higher duty than came under the head of medical etiquette."[6]

the field. Earlier, she had designed a modified officer's uniform for herself that she wore throughout her war service. In addition to the green sash, she wore pants with gold stripes, a felt hat with a gold cord around it, and an officer's coat.

In Fredericksburg, Walker became repulsed by unnecessary amputations of arms and legs. She had been trained to restore the injured limb, allowing amputation only as the last resort. Because the conditions on the battlefield were horrible, transport difficult, and infection common, many doctors believed amputations saved lives. Walker, however, began privately advising soldiers facing amputation that they had the right to refuse the surgery. She knew she would only face hostility if she confronted surgeons herself and reflected that it was her "solemn duty to the soldiers" to advise them privately.[5]

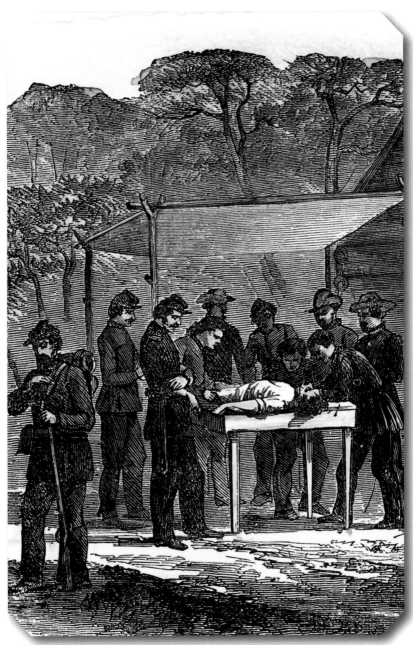

Medical and hospital facilities during the Civil War were often unsanitary.

Chapter 5

Union troops camped in and around Washington DC during the Civil War.

ON THE FRONT, BEHIND THE LINES

In 1863, Dr. Mary Edwards Walker was still without any official recognition from the army. She returned to Washington DC and pursued various community projects to benefit the families of soldiers. Doing so, she made a little money and kept herself visible to the officials she hoped to impress.

ON BEHALF OF OTHERS

One of Walker's projects involved helping the many women who came to Washington DC searching for sick or wounded husbands, brothers, and fathers. Because a woman traveling without a male escort was considered inappropriate, these women had difficulty finding places to stay. Walker raised money from a women's suffrage group in the city to rent a house, hire a manager for it, and turn it into a place of lodging for women. She named it the Women's Relief Association of Tenth Street. She also established a service to help women find their relatives in Washington DC's many medical facilities.

Walker tried to establish a private medical practice in Washington DC but had little success. Still, she managed to survive and became so well-known that many people asked for her help. For example, she helped soldiers receive furloughs, which allowed them a break from their duties. She responded to requests for supplies. She also continued to

An Educated Lady

In an 1863 column for *Sibyl*, Walker wrote: "I confess myself unable to see how respectable men can allow a laundress to go with their regiment, and shake their wise heads at the respectability of an educated lady acting as surgeon."[1]

help win the release of prisoners who were falsely accused of desertion, or leaving the army without permission. Walker was willing to approach the highest authorities, such as Secretary of War Stanton and the army medical director, to help the soldiers. She was known to never refuse a request for help.

Medical Care during the Civil War

Doctors in general were not well regarded during the war years. Soldiers dreaded being sent to dirty hospitals staffed by unqualified or drunken doctors. Medical care was appalling. The basic reason involved the poor state of medical knowledge. Civil War doctors were unaware of disease-causing microbes. They did not understand the links between mosquitoes and malaria, dirty water and typhoid fever, and unsterilized surgical instruments and infection. They knew next to nothing about antiseptics, and there were no antibiotics.

Rifles and bullets used in the Civil War caused horrible wounds that could become easily infected. Gangrene made soldiers' legs rot, and doctors knew no way to stop its spread other than amputation. Chloroform and ether were used to numb the pain of surgery. But when there were shortages, patients had to endure surgery without them.

Twice as many Civil War soldiers died of disease than were killed in combat. Contagious diseases such as measles and smallpox raced through crowded camps. Military operations were sometimes delayed because so many men were sick. There were not enough experienced surgeons in battle zones.

DRAWN BACK TO THE FIGHTING

Despite all this activity, Walker was eager to return to the front. She wrote to Secretary Stanton in November 1863, requesting permission to organize her own regiment with herself as surgeon. Certain male surgeons had succeeded with this strategy, but Stanton rejected Walker's request. However, Walker immediately traveled to Chattanooga, Tennessee, to help the thousands of wounded survivors of the Battle of Chickamauga, a costly Union victory. She arrived with a letter of recommendation from Assistant Surgeon General Wood, who had been sympathetic to her in 1861. But the doctor in charge refused to use Walker as anything but a nurse. She did stay long enough to win the notice and respect of General George H. Thomas, commander of the Army of the Cumberland.

With her usual persistence, Walker decided to approach President Lincoln for official recognition of her services. In a letter dated January 11, 1864, Walker asked the president for either an assignment in a women's ward of a hospital or, preferably, a surgeon's commission. She argued that she had been denied a commission solely because she was a woman and that she was eager to serve in any field hospital needing her services.

President Lincoln replied in five days. He wrote his response by hand on the bottom of her letter. He declined to interfere in decisions of the army's medical department, though he was willing to have her take charge of a women's ward if the department consented. Not long after this, however, a combination of factors brought Walker an official assignment at last. The assistant surgeon of the Fifty-second Ohio Volunteers at Chattanooga died on January 6, 1864. Desperately in need of more doctors, General Thomas, known as the "Rock of Chickamauga" for his heroism in battle, arranged for Walker to be hired as a civilian contract surgeon. She was to report to Colonel Dan McCook at Gordon's Mills in Tennessee in February.

Letter to Lincoln

In her January 11, 1864, letter to President Lincoln, Walker referred to herself in the third person. Walker wrote, "When her services have been tested and appreciated . . . and she fully believes that had a man been as useful to our country as she modestly claims to have been, a star would have been taken from the National Heavens and placed upon his shoulder."[2] Walker believed that men and women were not rewarded equally for similar service.

OFFICIAL AND UNOFFICIAL DUTIES

Walker still had a hurdle to overcome before she could get to work. Like most of the other civilian doctors who worked for the army, she was required to present her credentials to a board of military doctors. Walker's examination on March 8, 1864, was disastrous. The board declared her completely unqualified, doubted whether she had even studied medicine, and said she was suitable only as a nurse. Later, Walker insisted that the doctors had been set against her from the start. Although this failed examination did not interfere with Walker's assignment to the Fifty-second Ohio, it would come back to haunt her after the war.

General Thomas was not convinced by the board's findings. He ordered Walker to report for duty at Gordon's Mills. After nearly three years, Walker had finally received an official assignment. This was not a military commission, and contract surgeons were paid very little and usually overworked. But Walker finally had the satisfaction of holding a position that had never before been offered to a woman.

Regiment headquarters were in the home of Gordon, a miller. Walker slept in the kitchen along with Gordon and his family. The soldiers at Gordon's Mills were in relatively good health. The civilian population in the area, however, had suffered greatly from the recent battles. Families,

A "Medical Monstrosity"

After the war, one of the members of the examining board, Dr. Roberts Bartholow, wrote a letter about Walker's experience to a medical journal. He was as angry as Walker was, but for different reasons. Bartholow was offended that a surgeon's contract was even considered to be given to her, a "medical monstrosity . . . dressed in that hybrid costume."[3] He scoffed at her credentials from Syracuse Medical College, which he did not consider a real medical school.

many of which consisted of only women and children, needed food and medical care. Colonel McCook allowed Walker to travel widely, and she rode many miles on horseback. She served often in enemy territory. Walker performed simple surgeries and delivered babies for desperate Southerners caught between battle lines.

Walker sometimes stayed away from camp all night. Her appearance in uniform excited much interest. Once, needing a place to spend the night, Walker stayed with a family she had stayed with before. On the earlier occasion, she had shared a room with the family's daughter. This time, however, the mother told Walker that she was welcome to stay but must sleep alone because the neighbors all thought she was a man.

Walker was proud of her work. She felt she had converted some people to the Union cause, writing: "There is no doubt that General McCook's kindness . . . and my professional duties to these people caused a great many of them to abandon their allegiance to the confederacy."[4]

On McCook

In "Incidents Connected with the Army," Walker referred to General McCook as "a man of great sympathy and large sense of justice."[5]

A signed etching of Mary Edwards Walker, circa 1865

Southern prison camps during the Civil War were known for their terrible living conditions. Andersonville prison in Georgia had some of the worst.

WAR SERVICE ENDS

After two months with the Fifty-second Ohio, Mary Edwards Walker went too far into enemy territory. On April 10, 1864, she was captured and spent four months in Castle Thunder, a Confederate prison in Richmond, Virginia.

There is evidence that Walker had offered to spy for the Union as she traveled around the countryside looking for people to help. Although Confederate authorities found no evidence and never charged her as a spy, many people assumed she was arrested for spying. Compared with the amount she wrote on other topics, Walker wrote little about her arrest and imprisonment. Some believe this is because she was spying during her time in the Southern prison. In her letters, historians have found support for this view of Walker.

WILLING TO SPY

In September 1862, Walker had written to Secretary of War Stanton proposing that she be sent to Richmond to care for sick Union prisoners. While there, she would collect military information for the North. She even offered to wear conventional women's clothing if necessary. Though nothing appeared to come of her offer, events in 1876 later suggested that she did indeed perform work as a spy. When she sought an increase in her pension, the government turned her down. They claimed that she had not really served as a surgeon, implying that her true role had been that of a spy. The Pension Office wrote that she had been captured on purpose. She hoped to be sent to a Confederate prison, they said, where she could spy on her captors.

A historian of the Fifty-second Ohio wrote that many of the soldiers believed Walker to be a spy. Months before she went to Gordon's Mills, *Sibyl* published an article about her claiming she had offered her services as a spy to General Burnside sometime during the winter of 1862–1863. According to the article, he turned down her offer, but other generals agreed to Walker's plan. By the time circumstances seemed right for her to proceed, the new commander, George Meade, refused to allow her mission.

A later correspondence between General Thomas and Assistant Adjutant General Townsend also gives evidence that Walker was a spy. In a telegram, Thomas recalled that Walker had asked to join the regiment as a contract surgeon so she could move through Union lines and get information about the enemy. In his reply, Townsend asked what payment Walker might be due for her medical and spying services. Also, in 1865, a military judge claimed that Walker once got information that led General William Sherman, commander of the Union's western army, to modify his strategic plans. Walker herself never mentioned spying in her "Incidents Connected with the Army." She was a brave, adventurous woman, though, and may well have reported information to Colonel McCook and others about what she saw behind enemy lines.

RELEASED

On August 12, 1864, Walker was released after four months at Castle Thunder. She was part of a prisoner exchange and was proud to discover that the prisoner exchanged for her

Female Spies for the Union

A few women spied during the Civil War. Hattie Lawton worked for the Pinkerton Detective Agency during the Civil War. Posing as a male agent's wife, she went to Richmond, Virginia, to get information about Confederate army movements. Like Walker, Lawton was briefly imprisoned at Castle Thunder until she was released during a prisoner exchange.

Pauline Cushman was an actress in Kentucky, a border state with both Union and Confederate supporters. Accepted by the South as a sympathizer, she followed Confederate troops, reporting on their movements to Union forces. Cushman was caught and sentenced to hang. She was saved by the invasion of the area by Union troops.

Elizabeth Van Lew was an abolitionist and the daughter of a Richmond slave owner. Pretending to be a demented street person, she brought food and clothing to Union prisoners and sent information to the North.

Mary Elizabeth Bowser was born a slave. However, she became educated and was eventually freed. Bowser was placed as a maid in the Confederate White House by Elizabeth Van Lew, the daughter of her former owner. Because Bowser was assumed to be an illiterate slave, Confederate authorities spoke freely in front of her. She reported important conversations to the Union. She also read and passed along war dispatches.

Differing Views of Walker

One of Walker's biographers wrote: "To the men who ran Congress, to the functionaries of the government bureaus in Washington, Mary Walker, their frequent visitor and eternal correspondent, was a cantankerous, abrasive, harassing, professional scold who was perhaps insane; but to those who saw her tiny figure hovering over their bloody pallets in battlefield hospital tents, she was an angel of mercy."[3]

was a Southern major. This seemed proof that the government valued her. She and other prisoners traveled by steamship on the James River to Fortress Monroe inside Union lines in Virginia.

After the war, Walker would often lecture about her military experiences, but she did not often discuss her imprisonment. She also chose not to write about it in her "Incidents Connected with the Army." In a handwritten note placed with these papers, she explained that talking about this experience would consume all her time. She preferred answering questions informally from friends and members of the public. Walker focused her writing on her experiences providing medical care and assisting families. Her most important goal was to be seen as a legitimate army physician.

After her release, Walker did write a satire about her time in prison for a newspaper. She humorously called the prison "Hotel de Castle Thunder" and ended by thanking the president of the Confederacy for his hospitality.[1] But Walker's prison experience left her frail, thin, and often ill. Her eyes and vision were especially affected. This made it more difficult for her to practice medicine.

Walker did not go home after her release. After a brief trip back to her regiment to get her things and say good-bye, she returned to Washington DC. Here, she hoped to recover and continue her quest for a military commission. Her first term of duty as contract surgeon ended August 23, 1864. Shortly after, she wrote to General Sherman. She reminded him of her three years of voluntary service to the Union and asked that he award her a commission with the rank of major and a position at the Louisville Female Military Prison in Kentucky. She called this "simple justice."[2]

With the support of McCook and Thomas, on October 5, 1864, Walker was given a contract as acting assistant surgeon. The contract was signed by Dr. Wood, and it came with a salary of approximately $100 a month. The Union Army also paid her $434.66 for her services with the Fifty-second Ohio and as a prisoner of war. Her assignment was at the Louisville prison. This was not a military commission and did not come with an army rank.

Mary Edwards Walker wrote to General Sherman to remind him of her work on behalf of the Union cause.

She was still a civilian, but her new title was surgeon in charge.

Louisville Female Military Prison

The women's section of the Louisville prison housed mostly Confederate women arrested for spying and other crimes against the Union. Walker replaced Dr. E. O. Brown, who had supervised both the male and female prisons and now was assigned only to the male side. He considered this a move down and soon began harassing Walker in every way he could. The male guards and medical assistants resented and complained bitterly about working for a woman. Even the prisoners disliked Walker, because she imposed stricter rules than they had been used to under Brown.

But Walker improved the prison. Supported by the commandant, Lieutenant Colonel Hammond, she believed her task was to upgrade the prisoners' morale as well as their physical well-being. To do this, she put in place various new rules. She said prisoners must stop singing Confederate songs and making disloyal comments about the Union. She insisted that the prisoners keep clean, respect each other, and take care of the children imprisoned with them. She intended to supervise any family visits and punish inmates for disrespect. She reminded the inmates

Compensation

Surgeons in the Union army were ranked as majors and earned $169 a month. Assistant surgeons, ranked as captains or first lieutenants, earned between $100 and $130 a month. Contract surgeons, who remained civilians, earned between $80 and $100 a month and were called acting assistant surgeons. Army nurses earned only $12 a month.

that they received better food than most soldiers. A group of prisoners promptly complained about her, declaring they would rather have no doctor than have her provide their care.

Although the prisoners considered her too strict, male staff members said she was not strict enough. Walker did many acts of kindness for the female prisoners and staff. For example, she requested that three young women, one who was 15 and two who were 17, be released and sent home. She helped the woman who did laundry at the prison go home to be with her children. She gave the kitchen staff extra money out of her own pocket. Still, she was often resented, and her rules were not followed. When a new commandant criticized her, Walker wrote him an angry letter. She defended the reforms she had put in place at the prison.

Harsh Critic

About Walker's conduct, Dr. E. O. Brown wrote to Dr. Robert C. Wood, assistant surgeon general: "I regard Dr. M. E. Walker as incompetent to prescribe for the sick in the Female Prison, and would further state that her tyrannical conduct has been intolerable not only to the inmates of the Prison, but to myself."[4]

An Unhappy Experience

In "Incidents Connected with the Army," Walker described her visits to recovering Union soldiers housed in part of the prison hospital. She was warmed by their gratitude as she presented each one with a Union flag. But, overall, her time as surgeon in charge was painful. The prisoners did not appreciate her attempts to make them more respectful. Various male authorities and coworkers disliked her determination to live by her principles and dress as she wanted. Later, when Walker applied for a pension, her personal assistant testified that in spite of the hostile prison environment, Walker had always been kind. The medical director, Dr. Edward Phelps, noted that she had shown the same ability and spirit in Louisville as she had throughout the war.

Nevertheless, in March 1865, after six months in Louisville, a weary Mary Walker requested a transfer back to the battlefield. But the war was nearly over, and her request was denied. She was sent briefly to Clarksville, Tennessee, where she took charge of an orphan asylum and refugee home. Southern General Robert E. Lee surrendered to Northern General Ulysses S. Grant on April 9, 1865. Then, on

April 14, Abraham Lincoln was assassinated. Walker was ordered back to Washington DC, where her war service officially ended on June 15, 1865.

On July 4, Walker was in Richmond, Virginia. She celebrated the holiday alongside Northerners and Southerners. Wearing her surgeon's uniform, Dr. Mary Walker read the Declaration of Independence to the crowd. ⌐

President Abraham Lincoln was assassinated shortly after
the Union won the Civil War.

Andrew Johnson became president of the United States after Lincoln's assassination.

THE MEDAL OF HONOR

The war was over, but Dr. Mary Edwards Walker was still a fierce patriot who wanted to use her medical training to serve her country. Her next step was to pursue a commission as a peacetime military surgeon. Walker decided to appeal to

President Andrew Johnson. She wanted him to assign her as medical inspector to the Bureau of Refugees, Freedmen, and Abandoned Lands, which provided services to newly freed African Americans and white refugees. Walker also wanted the government to certify that she had been a legitimate army physician.

SEEKING RECOGNITION AND REWARD

Walker began by asking for letters of support. Throughout the summer and fall of 1865, friends and supporters wrote to the president on her behalf. Several military men who knew of her dedicated work for the Union wrote to recommend her. An official from the Bureau of Refugees and Freedmen urged Johnson to appoint Walker as medical inspector. The president was moved by all the evidence of Walker's service and her suffering as a prisoner of war. He wrote to Secretary of War Stanton in August, asking him how the government might recognize her. Stanton turned the issue over to the new surgeon general, M. B. Ames. Despite all the endorsements, Ames reminded the president of Walker's disastrous examination before the medical board in 1864. He did not think there was any precedent to recognize or reward Mary Walker.

In Her Defense

In her angry letter to President Johnson, Walker addressed her failed examination before the medical board in 1864. She argued that "the examination was intended to be a farce, and more than half the time was consumed in questions regarding subjects that were exclusively feminine and had no sort of relation to the diseases and wounds of soldiers."[1]

President Johnson, however, continued to receive letters of support. At the end of September, Walker wrote to the president. She outlined her army experience and defended herself against the ruling of the medical board. In October, Judge Advocate General of the War Department J. Holt ruled against Walker's petition. Although Holt believed Walker should not receive an army commission, he did feel her war work should be officially acknowledged. Holt included with his decision a 12-page handwritten report praising Walker's dedicated service.

MEDAL OF HONOR

In early November, Walker received her rejection letter, which claimed there was no precedent to grant her a commission. However, on November 11, 1865, President Johnson signed a bill presenting

Dr. Mary Walker with the Congressional Medal of Honor for Meritorious Service. She received the medal in January 1866. She was the first and, as of 2009, still the only woman to receive the medal.

The citation was signed by President Andrew Johnson and Secretary of War Edwin M. Stanton. It states, in part,

Whereas, It appears from official reports that Dr. Mary E. Walker, a graduate of medicine . . . has devoted herself with much patriotic zeal to the sick and wounded soldiers, both in the field and hospital, to the detriment of her own health, and has also endured hardships as a prisoner-of-war four months in a Southern prison,

The Medal of Honor

The Medal of Honor is the highest U.S. military award. It is known as the Congressional Medal of Honor, but it is actually bestowed by the president in the name of Congress. It symbolizes bravery and respect on the battlefield. The Medal of Honor can be traced back to 1847, when Congress proposed a special certificate to be awarded when a "private soldier distinguishes himself in the service."[2]

The Medal of Honor was created to motivate and reward brave wartime service, but there was no set procedure and no criteria to determine who should receive the medal. This led to odd situations. In 1863, for example, the medal was promised as an incentive to any of the 864 men of the Twenty-seventh Maine who agreed to stay and protect Washington DC, although their nine-month tour of duty was over. Three hundred agreed to stay. By mistake, however, all 864 men were sent Medals of Honor. More than 1,500 other Americans, including Dr. Mary Edwards Walker, earned the medal during the Civil War.

A 1940s version of the Congressional Medal of Honor. The design of the Medal has been altered numerous times since its inception.

while acting as a Contract-Surgeon . . . It is ordered that a testimonial thereof shall be hereby made and given to the said Mary E. Walker, and that the usual Medal of Honor for meritorious service be given her.[3]

Mary Walker proudly wore her medal on her lapel every day for the rest of her life. In 1907, she received a replacement medal with a slightly modified design. She wore both. When questioned years later about what she had done to earn the medal, her response was, "for going into the enemy's grounds, when the inhabitants were suffering for professional service, . . . and no man surgeon was willing to respond, for fear of being taken prisoner, and by my doing so the people were won over to the Union."[4]

STILL A CRUSADER

Walker tried to return to medical practice in Washington DC, but her attention was soon drawn to social injustices. She first took up the cause of nurses who were fighting to receive pensions and other benefits given to male veterans. She joined others in publicizing the women's plight. Walker pointed out that the $20 a month they were asking for was a pittance for women who had given so much to their country. In one petition, Walker added that these patriotic women should be allowed to vote. Several bills for nurses' pensions were introduced in Congress, but they all failed.

This campaign began a practice that Walker followed nearly to the end of her life. She often presented her cause to any individual, agency,

A Poet

Walker was always an ardent patriot. A poem she wrote after the war included these lines:
"When I am buried 'neath the ground,
Wrap that flag my corpse around,
Plant that flag above my grave,
There let it wave! Let it wave!"[5]

or branch of government. Her campaigns pushed for reform, justice, and women's rights. Women were entitled by the Declaration of Independence and the Constitution, she believed, to all the rights held by men. Responding to a personal appeal from Dr. Lydia Sayer Hasbrouck, Walker became a leader in the struggle for the vote and for dress reform. She continued to write for *Sibyl*.

PUBLICIST FOR DRESS REFORM

Walker attracted nationwide publicity for dress reform in June 1866. She was in New York and had stopped in a hat store. When her clothing attracted a crowd, the shopowner called the police to escort her home. Walker refused to comply and insisted that the officer take her to the police station. At the station, when asked her name, she invited the officer to read it off her Medal of Honor.

Afterward, Walker decided to make the matter a test case of her legal right to dress as she pleased. She filed charges of improper conduct against the officer who had brought her to the station. Later, she went to court and appeared before the police commissioner. She energetically defended her clothing. She told him that she was a physician, so her clothing was both practical and hygienic. She gave examples of the several prominent men and women whom she had met with while wearing her reform dress. She pointed out how they had treated her with respect.

The commissioner decided that the officer had escorted her out of the shop to protect her from the crowd, not because of her clothing. The episode was covered in several New York newspapers. Articles, often illustrated by cartoons, mainly focused on Walker's dress.

Walker welcomed the publicity on behalf of the upcoming meeting of the National Dress Reform Association in Syracuse. She was elected president of the organization and delivered the main speech. To the convention goers, Walker predicted that women would be voting in less than ten years and that they would hold public office. Models, including a large woman, an old woman, a little girl, and herself, wore reform clothing. She demonstrated this clothing was suitable for all females.

Punishment

Walker made many bold statements and predictions when she spoke at the Syracuse meeting of the National Dress Reform Association. She even proposed that Jefferson Davis, the former president of the Confederacy, be punished in a most unusual way. She suggested he be dressed in hoop skirts and made to do "women's work."

Finally, the organization officially thanked the police commissioner and the New York newspapers. In the association's view, they had defended Walker's right "to dress in a manner that comports with freedom of motion, health and morality."[6]

After she received the Medal of Honor, Mary Edwards Walker wore it every day of her life.

To support herself financially after the Civil War ended, Mary Edwards Walker traveled on speaking tours throughout Europe.

GOING IT ALONE

In September 1866, Mary Walker was invited to serve as a delegate to a conference in Manchester, England. She used the opportunity as the start of a lecture tour of England, Scotland, and France. She was paid for most of her speeches. This allowed her to support herself during her travels. She wore a black, knee-length dress drawn in at the waist with loose-fitting trousers underneath. On her lapel, she wore her medal. Everywhere she went, her dress, personality, and passionate views excited interest and publicity.

LECTURE TOUR ABROAD

In Manchester, Walker was a minor celebrity to the British press. She spoke about how particularly appropriate it would be for England, under Queen Victoria, to grant women equal rights. Friends who shared her views opened their homes to her.

Walker spoke at St. James's Hall in London about "The Experiences of a Female Physician in College, in Private Practice, and in the Federal Army."[1] Among other issues, Walker called for equal pay for women doing the same work as men—particularly female physicians. The newspapers praised her personality, her speaking voice, her appearance, and her dignity. U.S. and British

Walker on Her Education

Walker observed surgery at several British hospitals, noting the latest advancements in technique. To large audiences, she spoke about her difficult, lonely medical education. She recounted how she had studied books on human anatomy privately in her room because she had not been permitted to attend an autopsy. She recalled being asked why she did not marry a doctor instead of trying to be one herself.

medical reviews, however, were uniformly negative. Traditional male doctors still condemned her training and entry into the medical field. Male medical students in the audiences sometimes harassed her.

BACK TO THE UNITED STATES

When she returned to the United States, the country was busy with post-Civil War challenges and seemed uninterested in her experiences. Beginning in February 1868, at the age of 35, Walker toured the United States on and off for more than two years. She spoke about women's rights, the health effects of alcohol and tobacco, and dress reform.

When she was not lecturing, Walker devoted herself to the campaign for women's rights. She lived primarily in Washington DC, sharing a small house with suffragist Belva Lockwood. Walker and other women formed the Central Women's Suffrage Bureau. They lobbied Congressional committees, wrote newspaper articles, and published pamphlets. They collected petitions and organized demonstrations. When Congress was not in session, Walker attended conventions, gave lectures, and saw patients.

In 1871, Walker helped organize a mass voter registration attempt by a large group of Washington DC women. The marchers were joined by Frederick Douglass, the famous African-American orator. At the voter registration desk, the women were told that, by law, only men could register. At that point, Walker came forward and demanded the women be allowed to register. Her words did not persuade election officials, but newspaper coverage noted that her arguments were well received by her mostly male audience.

In 1872, Walker helped collect petitions from all over the country asking Congress to pass a law including women in the Fifteenth Amendment. Ratified in 1870, this amendment gave the vote to African-American males, although gender is not specified in the amendment. The petitions were combined to create a document 240 feet (73 m) long, with 35,000 signatures. However, nothing came of the effort.

The Petition Fails

Walker, Belva Lockwood, and many other women had high hopes for their petition to include women in the Fifteenth Amendment. They wanted to pass it along to a U.S. representative from Massachusetts, Benjamin Butler, who had been a Civil War general. At first, they had trouble locating him in the Capitol building. Finally, Lockwood presented the petition to Butler, who accepted it graciously and agreed to present it in the House of Representatives. The women crowded into the galleries of the chamber to hear the presentation, only to see the petition referred to the Judiciary Committee. They knew that action symbolized the end of their efforts.

Rejecting a Change of Strategy

Suffragists tried and failed to vote in the 1872 presidential election. Soon after, the Supreme Court ruled that the U.S. Constitution did not guarantee all citizens the right to vote. At this point, leading members of the National Women's Suffrage Association decided that mass attempts to register to vote were ineffective. They decided that change would require a constitutional amendment. Over the following decades, they courageously pursued a constitutional amendment, state by state.

Walker disagreed with her fellow suffragists. She continued to believe that voting was a right of citizenship and that an amendment was unnecessary. The Fourteenth Amendment, she pointed out, guaranteed the rights of citizenship to all people born or naturalized in the United States. She favored civil disobedience and mass demonstrations to wear down resistance. Her strong disapproval of the amendment campaign alienated most suffrage activists. Walker lost friends and support. She campaigned for her principles in print and in

Women's Right to Vote

The Nineteenth Amendment, which was ratified on August 18, 1920, gave women the right to vote. It declares, "The right of citizens of the United States to vote shall not be denied or abridged by the United States or by any State on account of sex."[2]

person at every opportunity. In 1871, she wrote that when women one day receive the vote, the United States "will be a whole Republic in reality, instead of being scarcely a *half* one, as it is to-day."[3] In her 1907 pamphlet, "Crowning Constitutional Argument," she outlined her beliefs. She carefully argued that the U.S. Constitution was designed to create a republic in which power lay in the hands of each citizen.

As the years went by and a constitutional amendment seemed more likely, Walker distanced herself completely from the national movement. She even argued against an amendment, convinced that her own logic was superior. On February 14, 1912, the 79-year-old Walker addressed the House of Representatives Committee on the Judiciary. She spoke to them at length about why women's right to vote was already in the Constitution and an amendment was not needed. In 1915, at 83, she told the New York State Constitutional Convention, "I am opposed to granting men the right to vote on the *rights* of women. It is an unconstitutional usurpation of power."[4] To Walker, it was wrong that men would vote in order to extend voting rights to women.

INSISTING ON DRESS REFORM

Another issue divided Walker from mainstream suffragists—her unshakable insistence on dress reform. During the late 1860s and 1870s, she often appeared with prominent women's rights activists such as Elizabeth Cady Stanton and Susan B. Anthony. She also maintained her leadership of what was now called the Mutual Dress Reform and Equal Rights Association. But fewer and fewer activists continued to wear reform dress. By 1869, both Stanton and Anthony had stopped wearing pants. They believed that the controversial clothing distracted public attention from the crucial issue of women's suffrage.

Almost alone among prominent feminists, Walker insisted on wearing reform dress because she fervently believed that traditional female clothing was unhealthy. She also maintained that her clothing was appropriate for her profession. Beginning in the late 1880s, Walker usually wore specially tailored men's clothes including a high-collared shirt, tie, frock coat, trousers, and sometimes a tall silk hat. But she never tried to pass as a man, as some women did to enjoy freedoms granted only to men. She claimed her own freedom to do as she pleased.

WRITING FOR REFORM

In 1871, Walker took a break from lecturing to complete a book she had been planning. She called it *Hit: Essays on Women's Rights*. The title *Hit* is never explained in the book. In chapters on love and marriage, dress reform, tobacco, temperance, divorce, labor, and religion, she speaks passionately about issues she struggled with personally. The chapters on love and marriage and on divorce reflect her lingering bitterness toward her unfaithful husband. She wrote from the perspective of a single woman trying to earn a living and contribute to the world, which was an unusual perspective at the time.

Hit

Hit: Essays on Women's Rights begins with a full-length engraving of Walker wearing a knee-length dress with a lacy collar over straight trousers. She wears her Medal of Honor, and her long, curly hair is pinned up at the back.

Walker includes four dedications. The first is to her parents. The second is to "the practical dress reformers . . . the truest friends of humanity, who have done more for the universal elevation of woman in the past dozen years, than all others combined." The third is to female physicians "and all women who are laboring for the public good. . . ." The fourth is to all women everywhere, whom she describes as "that great sisterhood . . . with their thousand unwritten trials and sorrows."[5]

Walker hoped her book would enlighten and empower women. She observed:

Everything that makes woman in any degree independent of man, and, as a consequence, independent of marriage for support, is frowned down by a certain class of individuals.[6]

Walker centered every chapter of *Hit* on the family, which was women's traditional sphere. For her, the goal of all reform was happy marriages and healthy children. She believed that unhealthy clothing, unjust laws, and the use of tobacco and alcohol stood in the way of this goal.

In 1878, Walker published another book, this one addressed to men. It was titled *Unmasked, or The Science of Immorality. To Gentlemen. By a Woman Physician and Surgeon.* It was somewhat of a morality guide for men. Walker discussed topics rarely addressed openly. Because she aimed to improve society with her book, she explained and diagrammed how traditional women's clothing caused profound damage to women, men, and children—born and unborn. She argued that men's unrealistic and demeaning view of women harmed all aspects of human life.

Women and Horses

In her chapter on dress reform in *Hit*, Walker frequently compares men's treatment of women to their treatment of horses. No good horse owner, she points out, would put a horse in an uncomfortable harness, tie its mane up, or obstruct its legs. Yet women were expected to dress in uncomfortable, restrictive clothing.

Mary Edwards Walker circa 1880

Chapter 9

Toward the end of her life, Mary Edwards Walker wore a men's top hat and coat.

BACK TO OSWEGO

Despite her fame, financial problems plagued Mary Walker throughout her life. She did not have inherited money or a husband's income. She was completely responsible for her own livelihood.

STRUGGLE FOR A PENSION

During Walker's imprisonment in Castle Thunder, she had been undernourished. This left her with poor eyesight. For this, the army granted her $8.50 a month, but that was not enough to live on. Walker believed the government owed her a reasonable pension for her wartime service.

Beginning in 1872, Walker campaigned every year for an increase in her pension. Congressmen heard at least 25 bills on her behalf. She flooded the War Department with testimonials, legal opinions, and petitions in support of her appeal. In 1876, the surgeon general verified her military service but insisted that she was assigned as a nurse, which entitled her only to a pension of $12 a month.

Walker reacted angrily, "This is false as I never had a position as 'nurse' and would not accept one as either nurse or bootlick any more than would any other officer."[1] It was not until 1898, when she was 66, that her pension was increased to $20 a month.

Hairstyle Reform

In addition to campaigning for dress reform, Walker also protested the popular women's hairstyles of her day. Women often wore their hair parted in the middle and pulled back in tight chignons, buns, or braids. Walker believed that these tight hairstyles were harmful. She advocated a loose, comfortable hairstyle.

Vindicated

In 1890, the Pension Committee vindicated Walker in her struggle to be recognized as a physician, not a nurse: "Had she served simply as a nurse for the length of time that she served in the higher capacity of assistant surgeon, she would . . . be entitled to a pension of $12 per month. Her services were much more valuable and meritorious, involving much more hardship and exposure, and resulted in greatly injuring her general health."[2]

MONEY WOES

Walker tried repeatedly to get a government job. Finally, in April 1882, she secured a job as a mailroom clerk in the Pension Office. This was the building where she had first volunteered her medical services during the war. With her usual energy and self-confidence, she immediately began correcting the inefficiencies she noticed. She paid particular attention to the way packages were handled. She ignored warnings that she was overstepping the terms of her employment. She was fired in July 1883. Walker appealed all the way up to U.S. President Chester Arthur but was not rehired.

By that time, Walker was in great need of income. In 1887, 1888, and 1893, she gave lectures for a Chicago-based agency that arranged tours of "dime museums," an early kind of carnival sideshow. This work allowed her to earn some money.

FAMILY AND FARM

In 1880, Walker's father died. He left her the unprofitable Oswego farm. Walker had endless arguments with her tenant farmers. She traveled a good deal; sometimes, she spent only about six months a year in Oswego. During the other months, she was often lecturing. When she lived on the farm, she could barely survive.

Fortunately, her older sister, Aurora, was a prosperous widow who loved her dearly. Aurora supplied Mary with food and other necessities, paid some of her bills, and helped run the farm while Mary was away. The two sisters enjoyed a warm relationship until Aurora's death in 1900. Mary's other two surviving sisters, Vesta and Luna, and their husbands cared for and helped her, too. But she always struggled to make enough money.

As she grew older, few people remembered Walker's war service or her leadership in the women's rights movement. People in Oswego gradually saw her as an odd, rather quarrelsome old woman in men's clothing. Neighbors recalled the large "No Smoking" sign in her house. She was occasionally the target of pranks. But nearly to the end of her life, she left her farm to fight for women's rights and other cherished causes. As a newspaper reporter wrote:

Walker Remembered

When she was a schoolgirl, Alma Lutz met Mary Edwards Walker. Walker spoke at her school about her service during the Civil War. Later, in a letter, Lutz wrote that Walker "was a very brave woman. . . . We are apt to forget that and remember only her peculiarities."[4]

[There had] always been about her something more than eccentricity. . . she had been characterized by a sturdy independence, of which her wearing of the garments she liked best, regardless of criticism or derision, was only one and not the most important manifestation. . . . Few people have ridiculed Dr. Mary to her face. . . . Perhaps it was because she had a sort of dignity, and because about her essential "goodness" there has never been any question.[3]

ALWAYS AN ACTIVIST

Walker kept herself in the thick of current events. In 1881, she declared herself a Democratic candidate for the U.S. Senate. In 1890, she declared herself a candidate for the House. The Democrats declined to endorse her. She spoke out against the annexation of Hawaii, U.S. expansion in the Philippines, and the purchase of Alaska. She wondered how the government could spend millions while many who served the Union during the war were denied their pensions.

Despite heckling and ridicule, Walker remained visible. She had broken with the main suffrage movement but continued to insist that women already had the right to vote. Along with many other women's rights advocates, she opposed U.S. involvement in World War I.

THE MEDAL WITHDRAWN

In 1916, as the United States prepared to enter World War I, the Medal of Honor Board announced that the medal Walker possessed could only be earned for bravery in actual combat. Furthermore, it decided to revoke the medals of those who no longer met the revised guidelines. Walker was among 911 people who were no longer considered medal recipients. In 1917, Walker was notified about this decision.

Walker petitioned the board, reviewing the highlights of her army career. She reminded them that she had gone outside Union lines to help Confederate civilians during the war. Surely, this counted as bravery in combat. She expressed her outrage at the government's attempt to take away an honor that was rightfully hers. She assured the board that she would never stop wearing her medal, and she never did. In 1977, 58 years after her death, President Jimmy Carter reinstated her medal.

Honors after Death

In 1917, Mary Edwards Walker's Medal of Honor was repealed. Nine hundred and ten others lost their medals for similar reasons. But on June 10, 1977, President Jimmy Carter reinstated Walker's Medal of Honor. This was largely due to a campaign led by Walker's great-grandniece, Ann Walker. The government agreed that had Walker been male, she would have received a military commission and kept the medal. The Army Board of Corrections determined that Walker's services to Union soldiers and Confederate civilians, combined with her time as a prisoner of war, met the criteria for the medal.

When her medal was reinstated, the Army Board of Corrections highlighted Walker's "distinguished gallantry, self-sacrifice, patriotism, dedication and unflinching loyalty to her country, despite the apparent discrimination because of her sex."[5] Today, Walker's medal is on display in the women's corridor of the Pentagon in Washington DC.

In 1982, the U.S. Postal Service issued a 20-cent stamp commemorating the 150th anniversary of Walker's birth. The artist who painted Walker's portrait for the stamp chose to depict her in a dress, a decision Walker would surely have disputed.

LAST YEARS

In one of her last interviews, Walker recalled meeting important people and providing medical care during wartime. She said, "But now I am alone with the infirmities of age fast weighing me down and practically penniless, and no one wants to be bothered with me."

However, she added, "It is the same experiences that have come to others, and why should I complain?"[6]

In 1917, Mary Walker fell on the Capitol steps during one of her frequent trips to Washington DC. On February 21, 1919, she died at the home of friends who were caring for her. She was 86.

Walker was buried in her black trouser suit with a U.S. flag over the casket, as she had requested. She joined her parents in their family plot in the Oswego Rural-Union Cemetery.

LEGACY

Mary Walker was one of the very few nineteenth-century women willing to challenge traditional male and female roles. She was a pioneering physician, a Civil War hero, and an early leader in the fight for women's rights. A lifelong opponent of the misuse of alcohol, she witnessed the ratification of the Eighteenth Amendment establishing Prohibition. This made it illegal to make, sell, or buy liquor. A year after her death, the Nineteenth Amendment, which established national women's suffrage, was ratified. She was able to see women wear trousers during the bicycling craze of the 1890s and in their wartime work during World War I.

Walker was a brave woman who sprung to the aid of the Union and Southern civilians during the Civil War. Later in her life she wrote:

> My reason for my acts has been a strong conviction of that which I believed was right. . . . I do not deserve credit for standing up to my principles for I could not do otherwise.[7]

Mary Edwards Walker was a determined physician and advocate for women's rights.

Timeline

1832	1855	1857
Walker is born in Oswego, New York, on November 26.	Walker graduates from Syracuse Medical College. She marries classmate Albert Miller.	Walker begins writing for *Sibyl*, a women's rights and dress reform magazine.

1862–1863	1863	1864
During the winter, Walker treats wounded and ill soldiers at Fredericksburg, Virginia.	Walker works in Washington DC for soldiers and their families. She helps with casualties of the Battle of Chickamauga.	On March 8, Walker is declared incompetent by a board of military doctors.

1861	1862	1862
Walker volunteers at the Indiana Hospital in the Patent Office in Washington DC.	Walker earns a diploma from the Hygeia Therapeutic College.	In November, Walker volunteers her services to General Burnside, near Warrenton, Virginia.

1864	1864	1864
In early March, Walker is sent to Gordon's Mills to serve as acting assistant surgeon in the Fifty-second Ohio regiment.	On April 10, Walker is captured as a prisoner of war. She is imprisoned in Castle Thunder, in Richmond, Virginia.	On August 12, Walker is released in a prisoner exchange.

TIMELINE

1864	1864–1865	1865
On October 5, Walker is awarded an official contract as acting assistant surgeon for the army.	Walker serves six months as surgeon in charge at Louisville Female Military Prison in Kentucky.	Walker's war service officially ends on June 15.

1882–1883	1912	1917
From April 1882 to July 1883, Walker is employed as a mailroom clerk in the Pension Office.	Walker addresses politicians in Washington DC on February 14 about women voting.	In January, Walker is notified that her Medal of Honor has been repealed.

1866

Walker is awarded the Medal of Honor in January.

1871

Walker publishes *Hit: Essays on Women's Rights.*

1878

Walker publishes *Unmasked, or The Science of Immorality. To Gentlemen. By a Woman Physician and Surgeon.*

1919

On February 21, Walker dies in Oswego, New York.

1977

On June 10, Walker's Medal of Honor is reinstated.

1982

The U.S. Postal Service issues a stamp commemorating the 150th anniversary of Walker's birth.

Essential Facts

Date of Birth

November 26, 1832

Place of Birth

Oswego, New York

Date of Death

February 21, 1919

Parents

Alvah Walker and Vesta Whitcomb Walker

Education

- ❖ Falley Seminary in New York
- ❖ Syracuse Medical College in New York
- ❖ Hygeia Therapeutic College in New York

Marriage

Albert Miller, married 1855, divorced 1869

Children

None

Career Highlights

❖ Walker was one of the first female physicians during a time when women were often prevented from studying medicine.

❖ As of 2009, Walker is the only woman to have received the Congressional Medal of Honor.

❖ Throughout her life, Walker was a pioneer for women's rights and a dress reform advocate.

Societal Contribution

❖ Walker was committed to the belief that men and women are equal.

❖ Walker paved the way for women's suffrage, equal rights, and dress reform.

❖ As one of the first female physicians, Walker demonstrated that women were capable of entering the profession.

Conflicts

❖ Walker struggled with the male establishment throughout her life, particularly with military and government officials.

❖ Walker quarreled with the leading suffragists over the need for a constitutional amendment.

❖ Walker endured ridicule and contempt by insisting on her right to dress as she pleased.

Quote

"My reason for my acts has been a strong conviction of that which I believed was right. . . . I do not deserve credit for standing up to my principles for I could not do otherwise." —*Dr. Mary Edwards Walker*

ADDITIONAL RESOURCES

SELECT BIBLIOGRAPHY

Graf, Mercedes. *A Woman of Honor: Dr. Walker and the Civil War.* Gettysburg, PA: Thomas Publications, 2001.

Leonard, Elizabeth D. *Yankee Women: Gender Battles in the Civil War.* New York, NY: Norton, 1994.

Snyder, Charles McCool. *Dr. Mary Walker: The Little Lady in Pants.* New York, NY: Arno Press, 1974.

Walker, Dale L. *Mary Edwards Walker: Above and Beyond.* New York, NY: Tom Doherty Associates, 2005.

Walker, Mary E., M.D. *Hit: Essays on Women's Rights.* 1871. Amherst, New York, NY: Humanity Books, 2003.

FURTHER READING

Furbee, Mary Rodd. *Outrageous Women of Civil War Times.* Hoboken, NJ: Wiley, 2003.

Joinson, Carla. *Civil War Doctor: The Story of Mary Walker.* Greensboro, NC: Morgan Reynolds, 2007.

Web Links

To learn more about Dr. Mary Edwards Walker, visit ABDO Publishing Company on the World Wide Web at **www.abdopublishing.com**. Web sites about Dr. Mary Edwards Walker are featured on our Book Links page. These links are routinely monitored and updated to provide the most current information available.

Places to Visit

The Congressional Medal of Honor Museum
40 Patriots Point Road, Mt. Pleasant, SC 29464
866-831-1720
www.patriotspoint.org/exhibits/medal_honor
Located aboard the aircraft carrier USS *Yorktown*, the museum features interactive exhibits that explain the origin of the Medal of Honor and what it stands for.

National Museum of Civil War Medicine
48 East Patrick Street, Frederick, MD 21705
301-695-1864
www.civilwarmed.org
Features interactive educational programs and exhibits related to the advances in medicine made during the Civil War.

National Women's History Museum
205 South Whiting Street Suite 254, Alexandria, VA 22304
703-461-1920
www.nwhm.org
The National Women's History Museum is devoted to preserving and displaying women's historical and cultural accomplishments.

Glossary

abolitionist
A person who believes that slavery should end.

asylum
An institution in which mentally ill people are cared for.

Bloomer dress
An outfit usually made up of a knee-length dress over long pants.

commission
A formal document conferring an official position or authority.

Confederacy
The Confederate States of America; the 11 Southern states that seceded from the United States and formed their own government.

corset
A stiff, tight undergarment.

dress reform
The campaign to free women from the heavy, restrictive clothing dictated by nineteenth-century fashion.

eclectic medicine
A school of medicine that taught nontraditional approaches.

furlough
A leave of absence from a duty or responsibility.

Medal of Honor
The country's highest military award.

pantaloons
Baggy pants.

pension
A regular payment to someone, often given as a reward for work or service.

petticoat
    An underskirt.

pittance
    An amount much smaller than what is due or expected.

precedent
    A previous occurrence of something that serves as a guide for
    how future occurrences should be treated.

prisoner of war
    A person taken prisoner by the opposing side during a war.

ration
    A daily food allowance.

reform dress
    Variations on the Bloomer dress, all including trousers.

sentry
    A person who stands guard.

suffrage
    The right to vote, or the franchise.

suffragist
    A person fighting for women's right to vote; also called
    suffragette.

temperance
    The belief that people should not drink alcohol.

Source Notes

Chapter 1. Prisoner of War
1. Mercedes Graf. *A Woman of Honor: Dr. Mary E. Walker and the Civil War.* Gettysburg, PA: Thomas Publications, 2001. 66.
2. Elizabeth D. Leonard. *Yankee Women: Gender Battles in the Civil War.* New York: Norton, 1994. 139–140.
3. Mercedes Graf. *A Woman of Honor: Dr. Mary E. Walker and the Civil War.* Gettysburg, PA: Thomas Publications, 2001. 68.
4. Ibid. 66–67.
5. Mary E. Walker, M.D. *Hit: Essays on Women's Rights.* New York: The American News Company, 1871. 32–33.

Chapter 2. An Independent Upbringing
None.

Chapter 3. Medicine, Marriage, and Dress Reform
1. Mercedes Graf. *A Woman of Honor: Dr. Mary E. Walker and the Civil War.* Gettysburg, PA: Thomas Publications, 2001. 11.
2. Mary E. Walker, M.D. *Hit: Essays on Women's Rights.* New York: The American News Company, 1871. 38.
3. Ibid. 38–39.
4. Charles McCool Snyder. *Dr. Mary Walker: The Little Lady in Pants.* New York: Arno Press, 1974. 28.
5. Mary E. Walker, M.D. *Hit: Essays on Women's Rights.* New York: The American News Company, 1871. 143–144.

Chapter 4. To Be of Service
1. Mercedes Graf. *A Woman of Honor: Dr. Mary E. Walker and the Civil War.* Gettysburg, PA: Thomas Publications, 2001. 13.
2. Ibid. 26.
3. Ibid. 34–35.
4. Ibid. 9.
5. Ibid. 40.
6. Ibid.

Chapter 5. On the Front, Behind the Lines
1. Charles McCool Snyder. *Dr. Mary Walker: The Little Lady in Pants.* New York: Arno Press, 1974. 38.
2. Elizabeth D. Leonard. *Yankee Women: Gender Battles in the Civil War.* New York: Norton, 1994. 129–130.
3. Ibid. 132.
4. Mercedes Graf. *A Woman of Honor: Dr. Mary E. Walker and the Civil War.* Gettysburg, PA: Thomas Publications, 2001. 63.
5. Ibid. 56.

Source Notes Continued

Chapter 6. War Service Ends
1. Mercedes Graf. *A Woman of Honor: Dr. Mary E. Walker and the Civil War.* Gettysburg, PA: Thomas Publications, 2001. 70.
2. Ibid. 73.
3. Dale L. Walker. *Mary Edwards Walker: Above and Beyond.* New York: Tom Doherty Associates, 2005. 22.
4. Mercedes Graf. *A Woman of Honor: Dr. Mary E. Walker and the Civil War.* Gettysburg, PA: Thomas Publications, 2001. 76.

Chapter 7. The Medal of Honor
1. Mercedes Graf. *A Woman of Honor: Dr. Mary E. Walker and the Civil War.* Gettysburg, PA: Thomas Publications, 2001. 54.
2. "History." *The Congressional Medal of Honor Society.* 15 June 2009 <http://www.cmohs.org/medal-history.php>.
3. Mercedes Graf. *A Woman of Honor: Dr. Mary E. Walker and the Civil War.* Gettysburg, PA: Thomas Publications, 2001. 79–80.
4. Ibid. 81.
5. Elizabeth D. Leonard. *Yankee Women: Gender Battles in the Civil War.* New York: Norton, 1994. 249.
6. Charles McCool Snyder. *Dr. Mary Walker: The Little Lady in Pants.* New York: Arno Press, 1974. 60.

Chapter 8. Going It Alone
1. Charles McCool Snyder. *Dr. Mary Walker: The Little Lady in Pants.* New York: Arno Press, 1974. 65.
2. Constitution of the United States. *Archives.gov.* 29 May 2009 <http://www.archives.gov/exhibits/charters/constitution_amendments_11-27.html>.
3. Mary E. Walker, M.D. *Hit: Essays on Women's Rights.* New York: The American News Company, 1871. 136.
4. Charles McCool Snyder. *Dr. Mary Walker: The Little Lady in Pants.* New York: Arno Press, 1974. 103.
5. Mary E. Walker, M.D. *Hit: Essays on Women's Rights.* New York: The American News Company, 1871. N. pag.
6. Ibid. 59.

Chapter 9. Back to Oswego

1. Mercedes Graf. *A Woman of Honor: Dr. Mary E. Walker and the Civil War.* Gettysburg, PA: Thomas Publications, 2001. 71.

2. Ibid. 12.

3. Ibid. 16.

4. Elizabeth D. Leonard. *Yankee Women: Gender Battles in the Civil War.* New York: Norton, 1994. 157.

5. "Dr. Mary Walker." *The Women's Memorial Foundation Office of History & Collections.* 1 June 2009 <http://www.womensmemorial.org/H&C/History/walker.html>.

6. Charles McCool Snyder. *Dr. Mary Walker: The Little Lady in Pants.* New York: Arno Press, 1974. 151.

7. Dale L. Walker. *Mary Edwards Walker: Above and Beyond.* New York: Tom Doherty Associates, 2005. 81.

INDEX

ABOUT THE AUTHOR

Bonnie Z. Goldsmith is also the author of *William Randolph Hearst: Newspaper Magnate*. For many years, she has written and edited materials for students and teachers. She took time out to teach English as a Second Language for six years. She lives in Minneapolis and loves cats, reading, writing, and traveling.

PHOTO CREDITS